The Battle of Fort Montgomery

A Short History

The Battle of Fort Montgomery

A Short History

by Jan Sheldon Conley

PURPLE MOUNTAIN PRESS
Fleischmanns, New York

The Battle of Fort Montgomery: A Short History
First edition 2002

Dedicated to those who fought and died at
Fort Montgomery

Published by
Purple Mountain Press, Ltd.
1060 Main Street, P.O. Box 309
Fleischmanns, New York 12430-0378
purple@catskill.net
http://www.catskill.net/purple

Copyright © 2002
by Jan Sheldon Conley

All rights reserved under International and Pan-American Copyright Conventions. No part of this publication may be copied or transmitted without permission in writing from the publisher.

ISBN 1-930098-35-9

Cover and frontispiece/title-page illustrations by Jack Mead
Courtesy of Trailside Museums at Bear Mountain State Park

Manufactured in the United States of America
on acid-free paper

5 4 3 2 1

Contents

Preface
7

Introduction
9

Events Leading Up to the Battle
11

The Battle of Fort Montgomery:
A Chronology
13

"A Wild Thicket"
29

A History of Support
31

Acknowledgments
36

Bibliography
37

"View near Fort Montgomery,"
Benson J. Lossing from
The Pictorial Field-Book of the Revolution, Vol. I, 1855.

Preface

DAVID ROSE was summoned to Fort Montgomery. He worried about leaving his family. He worried about leaving his farm. It would soon be time for the harvest. Hannah, his wife, assured him that all would be fine at the homestead. She would take care of the children. She would do what she and the older children could to tend the farm. David's country was in peril, and he answered the call to arms.

David lived less than a mile from where the Battle of Fort Montgomery would soon take place. He marched down the road from the Rose family farm, heading east toward the Hudson River to join the Fifth New York Continentals and the Orange and Ulster County Militias.

Hannah prayed that David would return to her shortly. She could hear musket and cannon fire ring through the valley. She knew the two forces were now engaged. The British were here!

Patriot forces repelled the enemy many times that fateful day. Surrounded and outnumbered, it seemed all was lost, but David managed to escape. He was determined to get home without being captured, and he made it to his farm, along with two other soldiers. Hannah thought quickly and remembered an abandoned stone shelter once used for the cold storage of food, up over a hill, away from the home. It was here that she hid the men from the British.

Her husband's attempt at eluding capture was successful, but Hannah would soon be confronted by enemy soldiers making their way up the road. They found her huddled with her children. The soldiers demanded to know the whereabouts of the men seen heading this way, and when Hannah refused to reveal their hiding place, an officer ordered her to be mounted on a horse with a noose around her neck. With her life and the lives of her children in jeopardy, she proclaimed, "I will not tell. My husband left his family and farm to fight for the freedom and liberty of his family and countrymen. To honor him, I will not tell of their whereabouts." With the children crying at their mother's feet, the officer relented, saying, "There has been enough bloodshed today, cut the woman down."

David and Hannah were my great, great, great, great, great, great, great grandparents. My grandmother, Georgianna Rose Sheldon, was raised on the Rose family farm and lived in the community of Fort Montgomery all her life. She told me this story many times. It is at the root of my interest in this important battleground. At last, Fort Montgomery is receiving the recognition it deserves thanks to a grass-roots movement and the interest and cooperation of New York State's Park Commission, and Governor George Pataki, to ensure preservation and allow visitation to the site.

Introduction

IN *The Battle of Fort Montgomery: A Short History*, I attempt to provide a general overview to pique the reader's interest, to generate continued support for one of the most important and significant historical sites in the grand Hudson River Highlands, and to serve as a reminder of what took place there and the impact it had on our history. It is confusing that the commanders of both the patriot defenders and the British and loyalist attackers were distant cousins and share the same last name, *Clinton*. I refer to the defending general, George Clinton, who was also governor of New York, as "Clinton" and to the attacking general, Sir Henry Clinton, as "Sir Henry." Please see the Benson Lossing map on pages 10, 18, and 19 for the locations mentioned.

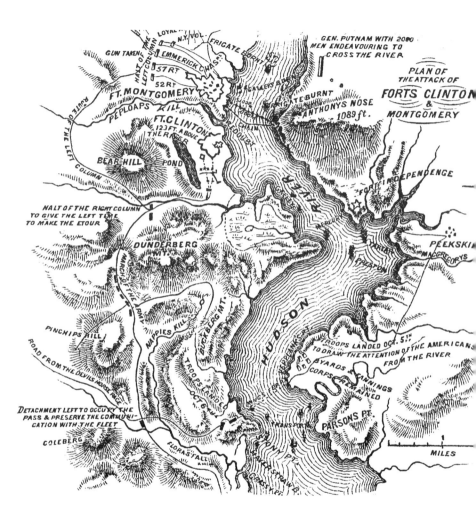

Map by Benson J. Lossing from
The Pictorial Field-Book of the Revolution, Vol. I, 1855.

Events Leading Up to the Battle

GENERAL GEORGE WASHINGTON'S Continental Army had suffered a series of disastrous defeats on Long Island and in and around New York City during the earliest part of the War for Independence from British rule. Washington retreated to New Jersey, and by a series of brilliant maneuvers, infused new vigor into the patriot cause. "They are all liberty mad again," according to a journalist of the day. Washington and his men were resupplied and reinforced by militia from New Jersey and New England.

After Washington learned that Sir William Howe, commander of His Majesty's forces, intended to lead an army from New York City to attack Philadelphia, he pulled a large number of his troops from the Hudson Highlands to defend his new capital, leaving his forts in the Highlands undermanned. Howe set sail for Philadelphia in July 1777 with 260 ships and 15,000 men, leaving his subordinate, Sir Henry Clinton, with orders to go north as soon as possible to rendezvous with British General John Burgoyne's advancement south from Canada. British strategy was to seize and maintain control of the Hudson River, severing New England from the rest of the colonies and preventing Washington's forces to the south and west from receiving supplies and men as well communications.

Control of the Hudson River was the lynch pin of the British War Office's grand plan, a three-pronged attack: Sir Henry would push north up the Hudson overrunning the defenses in the Highlands, General John Burgoyne, with 7,000 men, would head south from Canada attacking the forces of General Horatio Gates at Saratoga, and a third force would push east through the Mohawk Valley, under the command of General Barry St. Leger overcoming General Philip Schuyler and meeting Sir Henry at Albany, thus securing the river for the British.

Even though the patriots lost the battle for the Highlands, it was the heroic efforts of the men at Fort Montgomery and Fort Clinton, that may have saved the day and turned the tide of the war. A relative handful of Americans, who fought so valiantly, aided in delaying Sir Henry's reinforcements from joining Burgoyne at Albany and allowed Gates to gain much needed militia reinforcements in time to ultimately win Burgoyne's surrender.

The Battle at Fort Montgomery: A Chronology

October 1775

Thomas Palmer, a competent engineer, recommends installing a battery above Popolopen Creek in the Hudson Highlands, despite Bernard Roman's work already in progress at Fort Constitution on Constitution Island, opposite West Point, just five miles to the north.

January 1776

The Continental Survey Committee sends representative Lord Stirling to Fort Constitution. He discovers that work is progressing inadequately and reports this to General Washington. Work is ordered to cease immediately at Fort Constitution and all timbers sent to aid in the erection of buildings and ramparts at Fort Montgomery.

June 1776

George Clinton is appointed Brigadier General of the Militia and Commander of Fort Montgomery by General Washington. Fort Montgomery (named for General Richard Montgomery, who fell at the battle for Quebec the previous New Year's Day) is sited adjacent to the creek flowing through Popolopen Gorge.

(The gorge is such treacherous terrain that it is commonly known today as "Hell Hole.")

It is recommended that an additional fort be erected on the bluff across the gorge of the Popolopen after it is ascertained that Sir Henry could fire at will on Fort Montgomery from that position. George Clinton's brother, Colonel James Clinton, is appointed its post commander. The fort is called Fort Clinton.

July 1776
A secret committee appointed by the Provincial Congress, studies the river for the placement of an iron chain to obstruct British ships trying to sail upriver. Fort Montgomery is selected because the river is nar-

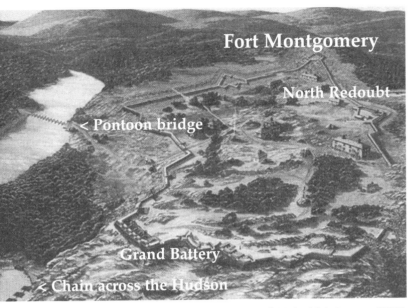

Drawing by Jack Mead with labels added. Courtesy of PIPC.

row there and the fort's cannon could fire easily on British ships approaching the chain.

August 1776

Clinton informs Washington that he has "taken the hilltop" and has militiamen, working "as if for themselves," fortifying Forts Montgomery and Clinton. Beacons and alarm posts are established up and down the river valley at strategic vantage points.

November 1776

The Great Iron Chain is drawn across the Hudson River from the Popolopen Creek on the western shore to the base of the Hudson Highland mountain known as Anthony's Nose on the eastern shore. The chain breaks twice and Lieutenant Thomas Mackin is called in to determine the cause. He finds no fault with the installation and believes it will be easy to replace once the ice leaves the river in the spring.

Spring 1777

Work continues slowly but surely on the forts of the Highlands. Authorized by an act of the Continental Congress, construction of the frigates *Montgomery* and *Congress* are progressing in Poughkeepsie. *Cheveaux de frise* are constructed and submerged well to the north of Fort Montgomery, near Polopel's Island. (These were basically "boxes of rocks" with spikes attached to be sunk in shallow water to puncture any vessel attempting to pass over them.)

July 1, 1777

Washington authorizes Clinton to call into service the militias of Ulster, Orange, Dutchess, and Westchester Counties for the defense of the posts and passes of the Highlands.

July 2, 1777

Brigadier General George Clinton sends orders to the militias to march to Fort Montgomery without delay. "The safety of the Continent may depend on it," Clinton writes.

July 7, 1777

George Clinton receives word from his brother-in-law,

Christopher Tappan, that he has been elected as civilian Governor of New York. He accepts the position, but stays at Fort Montgomery until August and then heads to his headquarters in Kingston, New York's first capital.

July 9, 1777

Some militia desert to tend their farms. A few are tried for desertion at Fort Montgomery and sentenced to fifty lashes. Clinton receives a request for more men from Colonel Hughes at Fort Constitution to guard the stores there. Clinton replies that he cannot spare any men, least of all to "guard salt."

October 4, 1777

A large body of British soldiers lands on the east side of the river below Peekskill hoping the patriots will expect a major attack from that direction. This ruse works. General Israel Putnam, commander of Fort Independence near Peekskill, is reluctant to send troops to Fort Montgomery because he expects an attack on his own fort. Despite the pleadings of Clinton to send reinforcements, Putnam thinks it wise to keep his men on the eastern shore. The British, in fact, attack up the western shore, and when Putnam finally sends troops late in the afternoon of October 6, it is of no use. They do not make it to the twin forts in time to be of assistance.

October 5, 1777

Early in the morning, Governor/Brigadier General George Clinton sets sail for Fort Montgomery from his headquarters in Kingston. He sees beacon fires and hears signal guns. Clinton marches on to Fort Montgomery.

Above: "View near Fort Montgomery," detail of the map on page 10, Benson J. Lossing from *The Pictorial Field-Book of the Revolution*, Vol. I, 1855.

Overleaf: "Plan of the Attack on the Forts Clinton and Montgomery upon Hudsons River" by John Hills, London, 1784. Courtesy of FMBA.

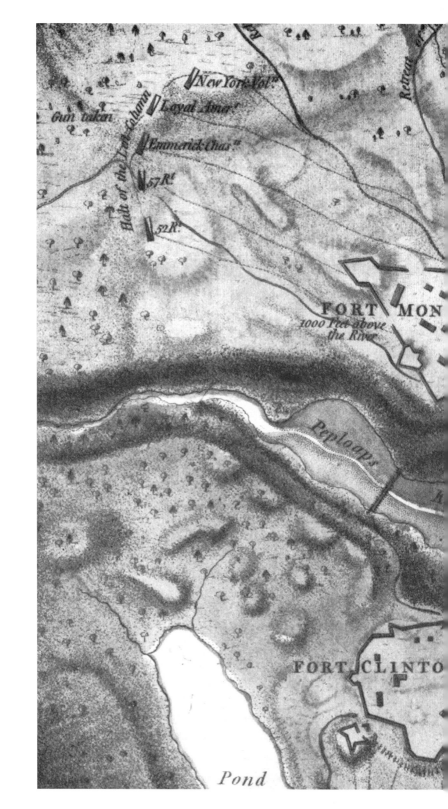

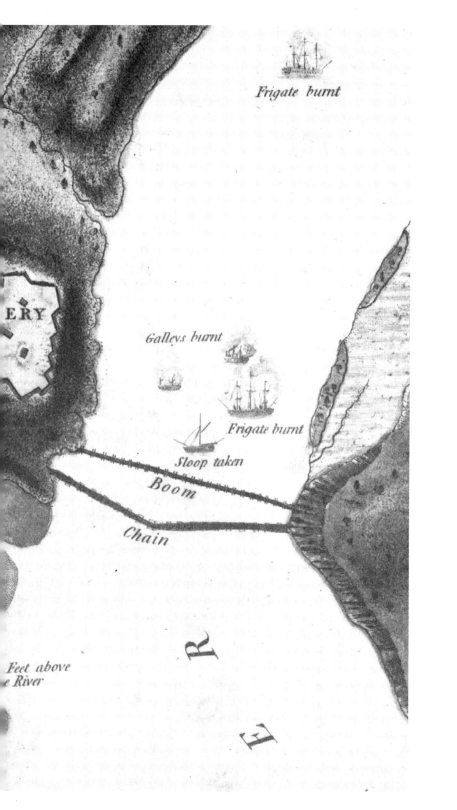

Daybreak, October 6, 1777
Clinton sends trusted Major Samuel Logan south toward Haverstraw to reconnoiter. Logan reports that he has seen approximately 2,000 British soldiers and upward of forty flat-bottomed boats land on the west shore with reason to believe that more were to come.

Under a cover of thick fog the British disembark at King's Ferry, just south of Dunderberg Mountain, a few miles south of the forts. The British forces divide near Doodletown, a hamlet nestled between Dunderberg and Bear Mountains, after marching through the Tymp Pass. Some 1,200 Hessian and other troops lead by Major General John Vaughan, head north and around the eastern side of Bear Mountain toward Fort Clinton. Another 900 soldiers, lead by Colonel Mungo Campbell, march around the western side of Bear Mountain, cross Popolopen Creek, and head east toward Fort Montgomery.

Morning, October 6, 1777
Clinton dispatches Lieutenant Paton Jackson and a small party south several miles toward Doodletown. This advance party is attacked at Doodletown by Hessians and returns to Fort Clinton. Clinton hears the firing from "Jackson's Skirmish" and orders the advance of fifty of Lieutenant Colonel Jacobus Bruyn's continentals and fifty of Colonel James McClaughry's militiamen toward Doodletown.

The battle begins to take shape as Colonel John

The British force included:
Lieutenant Colonel Mungo Campbell leading 900 men of the Fifty-second and Fifty-seventh Regiments of Foot

Major General John Vaughan with 1,200 men of the Grenadier and Light Infantry Battalion and several Regiments of Foot and Frasier's Highlanders, a dismounted troop of Light Dragoons and 200 Hessian Chasseurs

Colonel Beverley Robinson (a Loyalist from Garrison, New York) leading his Loyal American Regiment

Major Alexander Grant's New York Volunteers

Captain Andreas Emmerick's Provincial Chasseurs.

Major William Tryon, former royal governor of New York, also commanded a division of untold numbers

Commodore W. Hotham, Commander of the British Fleet, dispatched galleys and advance squadrons under the command of Sir James Wallace consisting of approximately six ships: *Crane, Dependence, Spitfire, Preston, Mercury,* and *Tartar*

Attackers total military personnel: approximately 3,100.

The patriot force included:
Colonel Lewis Dubois' Fifth New York Regiment from Ulster County

Colonel John Lamb's Regiment of the Continental Artillery

Colonels William Allison, Jesse Woodhull, James McClaughry and Jonathan Hasbrouck's Militias

The frigates *Montgomery* and *Congress*, two row galleys, and a privateer sloop to protect the Hudson River just north of the Great Iron Chain.

Defenders total military personnel: approximately 600, 300 at each fort.

Lamb's artillery is ordered to take a fieldpiece up the road that runs west toward Queensboro Furnace at the Forest of Dean Mine, near Torne Hill, to engage Campbell, who is leading his men east toward the fort. The patriots repel the enemy with grape shot from their fieldpiece and with musket fire. The attackers are repeatedly driven back before Lamb's position is finally outflanked. The patriots are forced to abandon the fieldpiece and flee.

To cover Lamb's men in their retreat, Clinton sends Captain Ephraim Fenno, commanding a 12 pounder, and 150 men west to Torne Hill. The fieldpiece is placed on a steep rocky slope where the hill falls away to the rapid waters below, the "Hell Hole" of the Popolopen. This plan of Clinton's works for a time. Campbell's men are thrown into confusion by the patriot cannon fire.

The patriots are finally outnumbered and outflanked, but not without first causing the British great annoyance. Captain Fenno's brave engagement foils the enemy for a time, although he pays for it dearly with his capture.

Clinton dispatches a message to Putnam making a plea for reinforcements. They are eventually sent, though too few and too late. They arrive across the river in the late afternoon.

Early Afternoon, October 6, 1777
British galleys and armed sloops now come up the

Hudson though the wind and tide are against them. The enemy approaches the fort and begins the attack. Men under Clinton at Fort Montgomery, and his brother James at Fort Clinton, repel the attackers again and again killing and wounding many, including some officers. The fighting, often-fierce hand-to-hand combat continues.

Brigadier General George Clinton
New York State Library

Late Afternoon, October 6, 1777
Lieutenant Colonel Mungo Campbell and several British regulars approach the fort with a flag of truce indicating that they wish to avoid "further effusion of blood." Clinton sends Lieutenant Colonel William S. Livingston to meet the enemy. The British officer requests that the patriots surrender. They are promised that no harm would come to them. Livingston, in turn, invites Campbell to surrender and promises him and his men good treatment. Fuming at this audacity, the British resume the fight.

British ships working against an ebb tide attack the forts and American vessels. A steady volley ensues with each side receiving a share of the bombardment.

British officers Campbell and Vaughan close in on all sides of the twin forts. Leading his men into battle, Campbell is killed in a violent attack on the North Redoubt of Fort Montgomery. Vaughan's horse is shot from under him as he rides into battle at Fort Clinton.

Dusk

The defenders are overpowered by sheer numbers and the British gain possession of Forts Montgomery and Clinton. Those who were not killed or did not escape are shipped to the infamous Sugar House Prisons in New York City and then onto British "hell ships" (prison ships) in the harbor. A "return," or report of prisoners, is sent to communities in the Highlands to inform families of their loved ones' capture. It is up to the families to send provisions lest the prisoners starve. Countless patriots perish on the prison ships.

On the patriot side: Colonel Dubois receives a bayonet wound to the neck but escapes. Colonel Lamb escapes unharmed, but Colonel McClaughry and Major Logan, both wounded, are captured. Thomas Machin is wounded, but escapes. Governor/Brigadier General George Clinton escapes down the steep embankment to the river. His brother James takes a bayonet wound in the thigh but manages to escape. Three hundred and fifty defenders are killed, wounded, or captured. On the British side: at least 190 are killed or wounded.

The patriots' small flotilla is doomed. The *Congress*,

commanded by Lieutenant Shaw, retreats north. She is run aground at Fort Constitution. Those aboard are able to escape and the ship is torched. The ebb flow of the mighty Hudson proves too powerful for the few men on the *Montgomery*, commanded by Captain Hodge. As the *Montgomery* drifts helplessly south toward the chain, Hodge accepts the futility of the situation and sets her ablaze lest the enemy take her. (The scene was described at the time as a "magnificent pyramid of fire.")

Nightfall, October 6, 1777

The British are in full control of the twin forts.

October 7, 1777

Clinton reports to the state legislature that he managed to escape by crossing the river to meet General Israel Putnam in Continental Village, east of Anthony's Nose. Clinton writes: "We have the satisfaction to be assured that all officers of the garrison fought like heroes, distinguished themselves both by their courage and conduct, and that all the privates, as well as militia, as [well as] Continental[s], fought with the utmost bravery."

Nineteen-year-old Major General Marquis de Lafayette, a trusted field officer and confidante to General Washington, comments to him soon after the Battle of Fort Montgomery, "This was indeed a terrible blow to the American Cause." Washington replies, "Do you think that in a contest of such magnitude there should be nothing but sunshine?"

Commander of the British Fleet, Commodore William Hotham, orders the great boomed chain cut, and the Royal Navy sails through, heading north up the Hudson. Hotham notes that the obstruction gives "strong proof of Labour, Industry and Skill."

The British fleet sails north as far as the capital at Kingston and burns it to the ground, but it is far too late to help Burgoyne, who has surrendered to Gates at Saratoga. The fleet retreats to New York City destroying the works at Forts Montgomery and Clinton.

Spring 1778

The British dumped the fallen Americans in a pond just north of Fort Montgomery. The horror of this scene is overwhelming, according to Dr. Timothy Dwight, a chaplain of the American Army, who visits in the spring 1778. He writes, "The clothes, which they wore when they were killed, were still on them, and proved that they were militia, being the ordinary dress of farmers. There lie the youth who stood in the honor of their country's trials; they fought and fell to purchase the independence of their country and there they lie without burial."

"A Wild Thicket"

NEARLY ONE HUNDRED AND FORTY YEARS passed before anyone took real notice of Fort Montgomery. The Palisades Interstate Park Commission (PIPC) requested an archeological survey, and in 1916, Reginald Pelham Bolton and Edward Hagerman Hall, representing the American Scenic and Historic Preservation Society, provided a report and made recommendations to the PIPC based on their visits to the site. In the report, they described the overall characteristics of the fort site, including ramparts, necessaries (latrines), barracks, a more recent dwelling, and evidence of excavation for iron ore. They noted that Benson Lossing visited the site in 1848 as he researched material for his *The Pictorial Field-Book of the Revolution*. Lossing found nothing but stunted grass and dwarf cedar. He made note of the remains of the battery. At the time of the report, the site was lush with growth and inaccessible without the aid of a hatchet. Hall and Bolton referred to it as a "wild thicket with pine, hemlock, cedar, cherry button, and other species of tree," many growing out of heaps of stone and old building foundations. The site was also tangled with underbrush and vines.

Bolton and Hall found gunflints, bullets, lead, china, glass, pottery, pieces of pipe, a buckle, some buttons, pieces of iron camp kettles, and an Indian flint spearhead. Additional Revolutionary War artifacts were discovered when a new state highway, Route 9W, was cut through the northwest portion of the site.

Bolton and Hall made many recommendations. These included conducting further archeological and topographical surveys; repairing earthworks and stone walls; reconstructing some aspects of the site; railing off foundations with iron piping; and placing suitable markings or placards to identify the foundations. They suggested using a large glacial boulder as an appropriate base for a statue of George Clinton and a tablet that would include the principal facts of the battle and a list of the names of the troops who defended the fort. They also recommended that a house be built for a local caretaker and a historical museum for artifacts and maps to interpret the site for the public.

Hall and Bolton's broad overview is remarkable. These two men were able to marry their technical view with an artistic vision. Obviously, they hoped to reveal the great significance of this tiny, wild thicket.

Although the site continued to languish, further archeological work was performed in 1935 and 1936 and again in 1958 under the direction of the Trailside Museums of Bear Mountain State Park.

A History of Support

IN THE 1960s, Jack Mead undertook new archeological work at Fort Montgomery. Mr. Mead was then director of the Trailside Museums at Bear Mountain. He conducted a detailed archeological dig with the help of Edward Lennik and others. Along with detailed maps of his findings, Mr. Mead presented the PIPC with drawings of his interpretations of the buildings that were on site at the time of the battle. One can view his fine paintings of the events of the battle at the Trailside Museum. The artifacts that he found at the site are inventoried and stored at Peebles Island in Troy, New York, by the New York State Office of Parks, Recreation and Historic Preservation.

In the 1970s, a group led by Donald Clark, then Orange County Historian, celebrated the bicentennial of the Battles of Forts Montgomery and Clinton. Dinners, activities, and news coverage brought public attention to the site. It wasn't until 1997, however, that a small group of concerned local citizens formed an association to help bring recognition to the Fort Montgomery Battle Site. Initially sponsored by the Town of Highlands Historical Society, the Fort Montgomery Battle Site Association (FMBSA) was formed and received its charter as a not-for-profit group in June 1997. The FMBSA was then able to solicit membership, collect dues, and begin the task of joining forces with the state to bring about official recognition.

Once the Palisades Interstate Park Commission was introduced to the association's ideas, it joined with the FMBSA in the clearing, stabilization, and interpretation of the site so that the public could visit for the first time in 225 years. What was once a "diamond in the rough" became a sparkling gem set in the Hudson River Highlands.

With the support of Representatives Benjamin Gilman and Sue Kelly, Governor George Pataki allocated a million dollars from the New York State Heritage Trails Fund to undertake the massive amount of work needed to finish the site. The PIPC used Hall's and Bolton's vision as a guide. The site is now ready for visitors. The Office of Parks, Recreation and Historic Preservation is to be congratulated for interpreting the site through handsome signage prepared with dignity and integrity.

Many thanks are due the groups that worked tirelessly for many years on behalf of this important site. It should be visited with great reverence for those who fought and died here for the freedoms that we enjoy today.

●

Facing page

Jack Mead led an archaeological dig at the site of Fort Montgomery from 1967 to 1971. He drew cut-away reconstructions of some of the fort's buildings based on excavated foundations. Top: Main barracks. Middle: Guard house. Bottom: Powder magazine.

Courtesy PIPC

Fort Montgomery today

Visitors learn about the fort and the battle from the site interpreter and informative kiosks at the Grand Battery and each foundation.

Photographs by Ted Spiegel

The Fort Montgomery Battle Site, just north of Bear Mountain and south of West Point, is open to the public as of October 6, 2002. For further information about the Fort Montgomery Battle Site, contact: FMBSA at: P.O. Box 376, Fort Montgomery, NY 10922; Town of Highlands Historical Society at http://www.highlands history.org; Palisades Interstate Park Commission at 845-786-2701.

Acknowledgments

I would like to acknowledge the following people for their contributions to this short chronology: Thanks first, to my loving husband, Stephen, who is my oak, my sweetest and most gentle critic. To our parents, Norman and Catharine Sheldon, and Charles and Grace Conley, for instilling in us a love of family, both present and past. To Karen Wilson, for her support always. To Doris and Garry Lent, Charter Members of the FMBSA; to Ken Krieser, assistant superintendent of the Bear Mountain Palisades Interstate Parks Commission and his assistant, Carol Nolan; and to Don Frasier, interpretive program assistant at the Fort Montgomery Battle Site for their critical review. To Alan Aimone, special collections archivist, USMA Library for his generous guidance and Susan Lintelmann, the manuscript curator, USMA Library, for her help with some of the bibliographical information. Suzanne Brahm, librarian, Highland Falls Library, for her attention and guidance. To Jack Focht, Trailside Museums director, for generously sharing his time and his memories of Jack Mead. To Herbert K. Donlan, Ph.D., for his many years mentoring the author. To Lincoln Diamant for his tact, grace, and editing. This short chronology surely would not have been possible without him. To Wayne Wright, librarian, New York State Historical Association Library, for the Benson Lossing illustrations and to Ted Spiegel for his contemporary photographs. Finally, to my publishers, Wray and Loni Rominger, and their copyeditor, David Hayden, at Purple Mountain Press. Thank you all for helping shape this book.

Bibliography

Calendar of the Historical Manuscripts relating to the War of the Revolution, in the Office of the Secretary of State, Albany, New York, Vol. II. Albany: Weed, Parsons and Company, printers: 1868.

Carr, W. H. and Koke, R. J. "Twin Forts of the Popolopen," *Historical Bulletin No. 1*. Bear Mountain, NY: 1937.

Clark, D. F. *Fort Montgomery and Fort Clinton*. Town of Highlands, Highland, NY.

Diamant, Lincoln. *Chaining the Hudson: The Fight for the River in the American Revolution*. New York: Carol Publishing Group, 1989.

Diamant. Lincoln. *Bernard Romans, Forgotten Patriot of the American Revolution*. Harrison, NY: Harbor Hill Books, 1985.

Donlan, Herbert. "Ten Historical Commentaries on Fort Montgomery," a collection of articles in *News of the Highlands*, 1996

Donlan, Herbert. "Fort Montgomery—Unrecognized." August, 1996

Kaminski, John. *George Clinton*, Madison WI: Madison House Publishing, 1993.

Ketchum, Richard, *Saratoga: Turning Point of the American Revolution*. New York: Henry Holt, 1997.

Lossing, Benson J. *The Pictorial Field-Book of the Revolution*. New York: Harber & Brothers, 1855.

Public Papers of George Clinton, First Governor of New York, 1777-1795, 1801-1804. New York and Albany: State of New York, 1899-1914.

Previously published titles in the Purple Mountain Press *Short History* Series

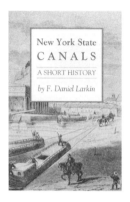  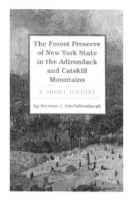

NEW YORK'S ERIE CANAL has long been heralded in story and song, and the legendary waterway is well known to people throughout the world. Far few, though, are aware of the fast 524-mile canal network that still exists in the state. It was the building of the Erie Canal during the first quarter of the nineteenth century that launched New York State and the nation into the canal era; arguably, no other enterprise was as responsible for creating the "Empire State." *New York State Canals: A Short History* tells the story of each of the state's many canals. 104 pages.

THE WEST POINT FOUNDRY, one of America's early ironworks, was built in the 1820s near the village of Cold Spring. It included a stone blast furnace to make iron from local ore and large water-powered lathes capable of machining large cannons. The foundry's best-known product was the Parrott gun, justly famous during the Civil War for its range and accuracy. 38 pages.

NEW YORK STATE'S FOREST PRESERVE in the Adirondack and Catskill Mountains is the only constitutionally-protected "forever-wild" forest in the world, but the Preserve and the large Adirondack and Catskill Parks are little understood by many. The short, accessible history answers every question. 39 pages.

New Yorkers in the Revolution is a Purple Mountain Press series of short biographies

DURING THE WAR FOR INDEPENDENCE, citizens like Marinus Willett truly risked their "lives, fortunes and sacred honor" to establish a republic in which they fervently believed. Willett's bravery and unflinching dedication to the cause of liberty made him a hero of Fort Stanwix in 1777 and saved the Northern Frontier for the patriot cause in 1781. He was a superb warrior, but the contradictions in his complex personality probably kept him from converting his military reputation to a successful career in New York's tangled politics. *Marinus Willett: Defender of the Northern Frontier*, 104 pages.

SYBIL LUDINGTON earned a place in American history on a rainy night in 1777 when she rode forty miles through enemy-infested woods to summon her father's militia regiment to halt a British raid on Connecticut and New York. This is the story of her ride and her life as a successful business woman in a profession then dominated by men. *Sybil Ludington: The Call to Arms*, 104 pages.

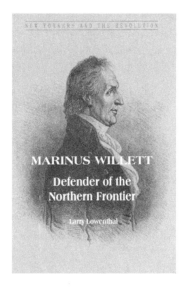
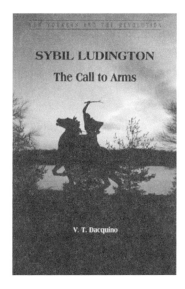

About the Author

Jan Sheldon Conley is a long-time resident of Fort Montgomery and a descendant of a militaman who fought there. She is a trustee of the Fort Montgomery Battle Site Association and served as its first secretary.

About the Publisher

Purple Mountain Press is a publishing company committed to producing the best books of regional interest as well as bringing back into print significant older works. For a fee catalog write Purple Mountain Press, Ltd., P.O. Box 309, Fleischmanns, NY 12430-0309; or call 845-254-4062; or fax 845-254-4476; or email purple@catskill.net.

http://www.catskill.net/purple